Armand Duplantis biography: The Life of a Pole Vaulting Sensation

Philip J. Ducan

Armand Duplantis biography: The Life of a Pole Vaulting Sensation

Armand Duplantis biography: The Life of a Pole Vaulting Sensation

INTRODUCTION

Armand Mondo Duplantis is more than a name; he is a sensation in the world of athletics, particularly pole vaulting. Mondo was born on November 10, 1999, in Lafayette, Louisiana, to an athletic family. His journey from backyard enthusiast to the best pole vaulter of all time has been nothing short of incredible. Mondo's father was a pole vaulter, and his mother excelled in several sports, so it was virtually inevitable that he would follow in their footsteps.

From the moment he took up a pole at the age of three, it was evident that he had a natural flair for the sport. By

Armand Duplantis biography: The Life of a Pole Vaulting Sensation

the age of seven, he had already achieved his first world record in his age group, kicking off a spectacular career that saw him smash records and win trophies at every level of competition. His early exploits included winning the World U18 Championships at the age of 15 and soon rising to international renown.

This biography digs into Mondo's life, examining not only his athletic achievements but also the factors that helped develop him into the champion he is today. It analyzes his development from a promising teenage athlete to a global hero who has broken world records and won gold medals at key tournaments such as the Olympics and World Championships. Behind the statistics and accolades is a story of perseverance, determination, and an unyielding ambition to push the limits of what is possible. Mondo's path is punctuated by triumphs and obstacles that test his determination. His

Armand Duplantis biography: The Life of a Pole Vaulting Sensation

dedication to excellence has inspired many young athletes around the world.

As we delve into Armand Duplantis' life, we will discover the factors behind his unrelenting pursuit of excellence, as well as how he continues to raise pole vaulting to new heights. Join us in honoring not only a tremendous athlete but also a true pioneer in athletics: Armand Mondo Duplantis.

TABLE OF CONTENT

CHAPTER 3: WORLD RECORD

CHAPTER 4:OLYMPIC ACHIEVEMENT

Gold Medal Performances at Tokyo 2020 and Paris 2024

CHAPTER 5: RECENT COMPETITIONS

Performance Analysis and Competition Results

CHAPTER 6: TRAINING AND COACHING

Training Regimen and Techniques

CHAPTER 7: PERSONAL LIFE

Influence of Duplantis's Upbringing on His Career

CHAPTER 8: MEDIA PRESENCE AND POPULARITY

Comparisons to Other Athletes

Chapter 9: FUTURE PROSPECT

Potential for Further Records and Achievements

CONCLUSION

CHAPTER 1: WHO IS ARMAND DUPLANTIS ?

The name Armand Mondo Duplantis is synonymous with athletic excellence, particularly in pole vaulting. His rise to become one of history's most recognized

Armand Duplantis biography: The Life of a Pole Vaulting Sensation

athletes is distinguished by incredible accomplishments, a unique upbringing, and an undying love for the sport. Duplantis was born on November 10, 1999, in Lafayette, Louisiana, and was destined for greatness from a young age. He grew up in an athletic household; his father, Greg Duplantis, was a former pole vaulter with personal bests of 5.80 meters, and his mother, Helena, was an accomplished long jumper and heptathlete. This milieu instilled a strong appreciation for sports and competition.

Duplantis showed tremendous talent from the minute he picked up a pole at the age of three, and the athletics community quickly took notice. By the age of seven, he had already established his first age group world record with a jump of 3.86 meters. This early achievement paved the way for a long and successful pole vaulting career.

Armand Duplantis biography: The Life of a Pole Vaulting Sensation

Throughout his childhood and adolescence, he consistently broke records, demonstrating his passion and determination. Duplantis' decision to represent Sweden in international events was influenced by his mother's Swedish roots. This decision would be essential when he began to make ripples on a worldwide scale. In 2015, shortly before his seventeenth birthday, he won the World U18 title with a 5.30-meter leap in Cali, Colombia. This triumph established him as a rising star in the sport, paving the way for even greater success.

As he advanced to senior-level events, Duplantis faced strong opponents while continually demonstrating his extraordinary abilities. At the 2018 European Championships in Berlin, he won gold by clearing 6.05 meters, becoming the youngest athlete ever to join the exclusive six-meter club, a landmark milestone that cemented his place as one of history's best pole vaulters.

Armand Duplantis biography: The Life of a Pole Vaulting Sensation

Despite his accomplishments, Duplantis had hurdles along the way. He initially enrolled at Louisiana State University (LSU) to pursue collegiate athletics, but he quickly discovered that his goals went beyond college competition. After only one year at LSU, he made the brave choice to become a pro and focus completely on his athletic career.

The COVID-19 pandemic created new challenges for athletes globally, but Duplantis used the time to hone his skills and prepare for future tournaments. His hard effort paid off in early 2020 when he broke the world record for the first time with a 6.17-meter jump at an indoor tournament in Glasgow. This achievement signaled the start of a record-breaking frenzy that would see him break existing marks several times over the next few years.

Armand Duplantis biography: The Life of a Pole Vaulting Sensation

Due to pandemic delays, Duplantis' biggest achievement occurred during the Tokyo 2020 Olympics, which were moved to 2021. He won gold with a 6.02-meter jump, realizing a lifelong desire and establishing himself as an elite athlete on a global scale. His performance was not only historically significant, but it also demonstrated his capacity to produce under pressure.

In future events, Duplantis proceeded to lift the bar,literally and figuratively, breaking three world records in 2022 alone. That year, he won both the World Indoor and Outdoor Championships, as well as several Diamond League medals. His accomplishments earned him titles like World Male Athlete of the Year and European Male Athlete of the Year. Duplantis' competitive energy is only rivaled by his modesty and devotion to his job. He frequently expresses gratitude to his family for their constant support during his trip. His

Armand Duplantis biography: The Life of a Pole Vaulting Sensation

parents were essential in developing his talent and teaching ideals that led him both on and off the field.

As he prepares for future contests, including the Paris 2024 Olympics, Duplantis remains focused on pushing the frontiers of pole vaulting while motivating future generations of competitors. His dedication to perfection demonstrates what can be accomplished with hard effort, drive, and enthusiasm.

Armand Mondo Duplantis is an iconic character in athletics, whose path from a little boy practicing pole vaulting in his garden to becoming one of the greatest athletes of all time is nothing short of inspiring. His journey is about more than just breaking records; it is about tenacity, devotion, and the never-ending chase of greatness, a story that will continue as he takes on new challenges and tries for even greater feats in pole vaulting history.

Birth and Family Background

Armand Mondo Duplantis was born on November 10, 1999, in Lafayette, Louisiana, which is recognized for its colorful culture and rich athletic past. His birth into a family with strong athletic roots will shape his life and profession. Mondo's parents, Greg and Helena Duplantis had a big impact on shaping his early experiences and instilling his love of athletics. Mondo's father, Greg Duplantis, was an exceptional pole vaulter himself.

He participated at the collegiate level for the University of Louisiana in Lafayette, setting personal bests of 5.80 meters during his career. Greg's athletic background gave Mondo both a role model and a mentor who knew the sport's complexities. Mondo learned the skills, training regimens, and mental components of pole vaulting from his father at a young age. Greg's excitement for the sport was contagious, and he frequently related anecdotes from his competitions, creating in Mondo a sense of desire and motivation.

Mondo's mother, Helena Duplantis, also contributed her athletic abilities to the family dynamic. Helena, a former heptathlete and long jumper, competed for Sweden in international competitions as a youth. Her diversified

Armand Duplantis biography: The Life of a Pole Vaulting Sensation

sports background helped create a well-rounded environment in which physical health and competition were highly prized. Helena's Swedish origin would eventually influence Mondo's decision to represent Sweden on the international stage, emphasizing the significance of both sides of his family history.

 Growing up in this active family, Mondo was encouraged to try new activities. His early life was packed with activities that helped him develop his physical ability, including soccer, baseball, gymnastics, and track and field. This exposure to several athletic disciplines provided him with a solid foundation of coordination and agility, which would serve him well as he progressed into more specialized training. The Duplantis family prioritized education alongside athletics.

Armand Duplantis biography: The Life of a Pole Vaulting Sensation

Both parents emphasized in Mondo the value of balancing academics and sports, a notion that he followed throughout his formative years. They encouraged his enthusiasm for pole vaulting while also supporting his academic aspirations, ensuring that he recognized the importance of hard effort in both the classroom and on the field. Mondo grew up in a close-knit familial atmosphere that emphasized encouragement and support. His older brother Andreas and younger sister Johanna were also active in athletics, fostering a competitive yet supportive environment at home.

Athletics was a common theme in family trips, whether it was competing or participating in friendly sporting events among themselves. This competitive mentality instilled in Mondo resilience and tenacity as he learned to deal with both successes and setbacks. As Mondo

Armand Duplantis biography: The Life of a Pole Vaulting Sensation

proceeded through school, he became known for his remarkable pole vaulting abilities. His inherent skill was evident even at an early age; by the age of seven, he had already set records for his age group.

The family's dedication to developing this potential became clear as they sought out coaching opportunities and training facilities to assist him improve his abilities. In addition to their on-field assistance, Greg and Helena highlighted the significance of mental strength. They taught Mondo how to handle pressure, which is a crucial ability for any athlete striving for greatness. This guidance became especially important as he began competing at higher levels, where expectations grew.

The Duplantis family's link to Sweden also influenced Mondo's athletic persona. Helena is Swedish, therefore they would frequently visit her native country during the

Armand Duplantis biography: The Life of a Pole Vaulting Sensation

summer and holidays. These excursions allowed Mondo to reconnect with his Swedish background while also exposing him to other sporting cultures and training systems found throughout Europe. During these travels, he first felt the excitement of competing against international competitors, giving him a taste of what was to come.

As Mondo reached high school at Lafayette High School in Louisiana, he continued to perform academically while also improving his pole vaulting talents under the tutelage of coaches who saw his potential. His performances at local meetings rapidly drew the attention of college scouts nationwide. Mondo's decision to represent Sweden internationally arose from both personal pride in his ethnicity and practical considerations for competing prospects.

Armand Duplantis biography: The Life of a Pole Vaulting Sensation

By opting to compete for Sweden, he opened up opportunities to display his talent on greater stages while also contributing to Sweden's burgeoning athletic reputation. Throughout his childhood, Mondo's family was instrumental in providing emotional support during both accomplishments and challenges. They celebrated each success together while also guiding him through disappointments, lessons that would eventually influence not only his athletic career but also his personality as a whole. As he moved from high school to elite-level competition, Mondo brought with him not just the abilities required for success, but also the values instilled by his family: hard effort, resilience, humility, and respect for others, qualities that have characterized him as an athlete and a person.

Armand Mondo Duplantis' birthplace and family history are critical elements of his biography. Growing up in an

Armand Duplantis biography: The Life of a Pole Vaulting Sensation

athletic atmosphere gave him unique possibilities that helped build his career as one of history's greatest pole vaulters. Mondo grew up with supportive parents who valued education and sportsmanship, as well as siblings who had similar interests, to become an athlete capable of achieving great exploits while being anchored in ideals that extend beyond the world of athletics. His family's legacy lives on as he strives for new heights in pole vaulting while encouraging future generations.

·

Early Athletic Influences and Beginnings in Pole Vaulting

Armand Mondo Duplantis' athletic career began at a very young age, formed by a unique combination of familial influence, early exposure to many sports, and an innate knack for pole vaulting. Mondo grew up in Lafayette, Louisiana, in an atmosphere that encouraged athletic accomplishment. His father, Greg Duplantis, was a former collegiate pole vaulter, while his mother, Helena, was a heptathlete and volleyball player.

This strong athletic tradition provided Mondo with the solid support and inspiration he needed to accomplish his own athletic goals. Mondo has a natural desire to be physically active since he was able to walk. At the age of four, he tried pole vaulting for the first time in his living room, using a makeshift landing cushion made of a couch. This early exploration was more than simply play; it foreshadowed his future as a world-class athlete.

Recognizing his excitement and talent, his parents built pole vault equipment in their backyard, allowing him to practice and improve his skills in a more structured setting. Mondo's early engagement in athletics extended beyond pole vaulting. He played in a variety of sports, including soccer and baseball, which helped him develop important qualities like coordination, agility, and competitive spirit.

However, pole vaulting captivated his heart and creativity. The exhilaration of soaring through the air drew him in, and he rapidly began to focus on learning this difficult skill. Mondo established his first world record for his age group with a leap of 3.86 meters (12

Armand Duplantis biography: The Life of a Pole Vaulting Sensation

feet 8 inches) when he was seven years old. This accomplishment signaled the start of a string of record-breaking performances that would define his young career. His ability to break previous records at such a young age grabbed the attention of both coaches and athletes, paving the way for his future success in the sport.

The Duplantis family's support for athletics went beyond simply encouragement; they actively participated in Mondo's training and development. Greg Duplantis took on the role of technical coach, teaching his son pole vaulting skills and ideas. This father-son dynamic fostered a close bond based on mutual respect and a shared enthusiasm for the sport. Helena also served as Mondo's trainer, ensuring that he remained physically strong while managing academics and athletics.

Armand Duplantis biography: The Life of a Pole Vaulting Sensation

As Mondo advanced through school, he continued to set records at local meetings and contests. His performances were frequently distinguished by a blend of technical proficiency and raw athleticism. Coaches saw his talent early on and sought to cultivate it by offering specific training chances. Mondo's extraordinary work ethic became apparent as he spent endless hours perfecting his technique and enhancing his performance.

In addition to parental backing, Mondo drew inspiration from existing athletes in the sport. Renaud Lavillenie, the French pole vaulting champion who had won numerous international medals, was one such influence. Mondo appreciated Lavillenie's approach and technique, and their first meeting in 2013 had a lasting impact on him. The event inspired Mondo to replicate Lavillenie's approach to pole vaulting while simultaneously creating

Armand Duplantis biography: The Life of a Pole Vaulting Sensation

his distinct style, which would later distinguish him apart from his opponents.

Mondo's decision to represent Sweden internationally arose from both personal pride in his ethnicity and practical considerations for competing prospects. With dual citizenship due to his mother's Swedish ancestry, he could compete for Sweden or the United States. Ultimately, he chose Sweden, encouraged by pleasant memories given by his older brother Andreas in youth contests representing Sweden. Mondo competed in the World U18 Championships in Cali, Colombia, in 2015, at the age of 15. His triumph there constituted a watershed moment in his early career, as he cleared 5.30 meters (17 feet 4 inches) to claim gold.

This achievement not only confirmed his standing as one of the world's best young athletes but also anticipated what was to come. Mondo's early athletic influences included not only family members and famous sportsmen but also coaches who saw his talent and guided him through important periods of development. The support network surrounding him created an environment conducive to growth, allowing him to experiment with techniques without fear of failure.

The combination of natural talent and family support produced an environment in which Mondo felt emboldened to push the boundaries of pole vaulting. His early experiences laid the framework for future success, imparting traits like tenacity and determination that he would use throughout his career. As he entered high school at Lafayette High School in Louisiana, Mondo continued to set records both indoors and outdoors, attracting attention from college scouts across the country.

Armand Duplantis biography: The Life of a Pole Vaulting Sensation

His performances were constantly excellent; throughout this period, he set national freshman records, demonstrating not only raw potential but also an unyielding devotion to perfection. In conclusion, Armand Mondo Duplantis' early athletic influences helped shape him into one of the greatest pole vaulters in history. Born into an athletically minded family that valued sportsmanship with academics he with unique opportunities for development from a young age.

His path began with basic home explorations and progressed to record-breaking performances on international venues, all powered by a passion for pole vaulting nourished by familial support and coaching from experienced coaches in the sport. As he continues to reach new heights in athletics today, both literally through vaults cleared above high bars, his beginnings serve as a reminder that excellence frequently emerges from humble beginnings anchored firmly within supportive environments and with a love for the sport itself.

CHAPTER 2:CAREER MILESTONE

Armand Mondo Duplantis' rise in the world of athletics is highlighted by a string of outstanding junior accomplishments that established the groundwork for his future success as a pole vaulter. His early achievements not only demonstrated his exceptional talent but also his potential to become one of the best athletes in the sport's history.Mondo continuously achieved new records and received plaudits throughout his adolescence, cementing his position as a formidable force in pole vaulting.

At the age of 15, Mondo competed in the 2015 World U18 Championships in Cali, Colombia, which was one of his first notable achievements. In this tournament, he made headlines by clearing a remarkable height of 5.30 meters (17 feet 4 inches), winning the gold medal and establishing himself as one of the sport's top emerging prospects. This triumph was significant not only because of his age but also because it made him the youngest athlete to win a world championship in pole vaulting at the time.

Mondo's performance at this event foreshadowed what was to come, as he exhibited both technical ability and mental strength under duress. Mondo continued to perform well on the junior circuit after his World U18 Championship victory. In 2016, he competed at the IAAF World U20 Championships in Bydgoszcz, Poland, where he once again demonstrated his exceptional ability. Mondo won another gold medal by clearing 5.50

Armand Duplantis biography: The Life of a Pole Vaulting Sensation

meters (18 feet 0.5 inches) in front of some of the world's greatest young athletes.

This achievement not only added to his expanding list of accomplishments but also established him as a strong competitor in future senior championships. In addition to international championships, Mondo excelled in national tournaments throughout his adolescence. He competed in high school meets throughout Louisiana and consistently won the pole vault events. His accomplishments frequently included clearing heights higher than those reached by older opponents, showing his great talent. During this period, he achieved numerous state records and was named one of the top high school athletes in the United States.

One of the highlights of Mondo's junior career came during the 2017 indoor season when he competed in the

Armand Duplantis biography: The Life of a Pole Vaulting Sensation

renowned New Balance Indoor Nationals in New York City. In this tournament, he jumped a staggering 5.80 meters (19 feet 0.25 inches), making him not only the winner but also the first high school athlete to clear that height indoors. This feat was monumental since it elevated him to an elite company and demonstrated his capacity to execute at an excellent level under difficult circumstances.

Mondo's success extended to outdoor contests as well. In June 2018, he competed at the USATF Junior Championships in Sacramento, California, where he won gold and earned a ticket on Team USA for the Pan American U20 Championships later that summer. His success at these championships cemented his position as one of the most promising teenage pole vaulters.

Armand Duplantis biography: The Life of a Pole Vaulting Sensation

Throughout these early years, Mondo's commitment to training and growth was clear. He worked hard with coaches who saw his potential and provided personalized advice to help him improve his technique and maximize his performance. His dedication to brilliance was bolstered by a strong network of family members who encouraged him every step of the way. As Mondo advanced from junior to senior tournaments, he continued to break records that had been held for years. His ability to continuously set new personal bests while competing against older and more experienced athletes revealed not only his physical abilities but also his mental toughness, a necessary trait for success in high-pressure situations.

During these formative years, Mondo's character shone through with his athletic exploits.Despite his growing recognition and awards, he remained humble and

Armand Duplantis biography: The Life of a Pole Vaulting Sensation

frequently thanked his family and instructors for their constant support throughout his career. This humility drew him to both fans and competitors, positioning him as a role model for future athletes. Scouts and coaches from collegiate teams across the United States were impressed by Mondo's junior-level performances. His remarkable track record sparked strong interest from renowned universities looking to recruit him for their track and field teams.However, after much thought and conversation with his family, Mondo opted to pursue professional athletics rather than compete at the varsity level.

As he entered professional competition, Mondo brought not just a wealth of expertise, but also a legacy built on determination and hard effort in his junior years. The records he set at this time would serve as benchmarks for

Armand Duplantis biography: The Life of a Pole Vaulting Sensation

future generations of pole vaulters, encouraging countless young athletes throughout the world.

Armand Mondo Duplantis' junior successes show a spectacular career defined by record-breaking performances and substantial accolades that cemented his place as one of pole vaulting's brightest lights. Mondo's early career provided the groundwork for future success on greater venues, with gold medals at international championships and unparalleled heights indoors and outdoors.

His journey through junior athletics demonstrates how skill and perseverance can lead to exceptional achievements, a story that continues to unfold as he aspires for greatness in the sport today.

Transition to Professional Athletics

Armand Mondo Duplantis' shift from junior contests to
professional athletics constituted a watershed moment in
his career, propelling him to the pinnacle of pole vaulting
and redefining the sport's standards. This transfer was
more than just a change in status; it was a deliberate
decision based on his outstanding talent, growing
reputation, and desire to compete at the highest levels
without the limits of collegiate eligibility.

Armand Duplantis biography: The Life of a Pole Vaulting Sensation

Following an incredible junior career full of record-breaking achievements and honors, Mondo enrolled at Louisiana State University (LSU) in 2018, where he continued to flourish as a pole vaulter. During his freshman year, he quickly established himself by setting a collegiate record of 6.00 meters (19 feet 8.25 inches) at the SEC Outdoor Championships. His performance helped LSU win its first SEC Outdoor Track and Field Championship since 1990, demonstrating both his talent and his ability to contribute to team success.

Despite these triumphs, Mondo's tenure at LSU was limited; he understood that his talent went well beyond collegiate competition. Mondo decided to turn professional in June 2019, following only one year at LSU. This statement came as no surprise to those who had witnessed his remarkable rise through the junior

Armand Duplantis biography: The Life of a Pole Vaulting Sensation

ranks. His decision to forego remaining NCAA eligibility stemmed from a desire to focus solely on his athletic career and pursue options that would allow him to compete on a worldwide scale.

The decision also indicated Mondo's confidence in his ability and belief that he could compete at the highest levels of the sport. Mondo's transition to professional athletics provided new chances for him, such as sponsorship and access to elite training facilities. He contracted with PUMA, a leading sportswear business, which offered him not just financial support but also tools to help him improve his training regimen. This collaboration allowed him to focus on fine-tuning his technique and enhancing his performance without the distractions that come with collegiate athletics.

Armand Duplantis biography: The Life of a Pole Vaulting Sensation

Mondo's first major international tournament as a professional athlete was at the 2019 World Championships in Doha, Qatar. Mondo had considerable pressure when competing against seasoned athletes like American Sam Kendricks, but rose to the situation, winning the silver medal with a jump of 5.97 meters (19 feet 7 inches). This performance not only reaffirmed his decision to become a professional but also established him as a major contender in the global arena.

The transition from junior to professional athletics was not without hurdles. Mondo had to adjust to the higher level of competition and expectations that come with being a professional athlete. The pressure to perform consistently at high levels might be overwhelming; but, Mondo's great mental fortitude, honed over years of competitive experience, suited him well throughout this transition phase. In early 2020, just months after

Armand Duplantis biography: The Life of a Pole Vaulting Sensation

establishing himself as a professional athlete, Mondo demonstrated his tremendous skill by breaking the world indoor pole vaulting record with a jump of 6.17 meters (20 feet 3 inches) at an indoor tournament in Glasgow.

This effort marked his first world record and launched a string of record-breaking performances that would define his future career. The jump not only cemented his place as one of history's greatest pole vaulters but also indicated that he was capable of breaking previously unthinkable records. As Mondo continued to smash records and win championships in 2020 and beyond, he gained recognition as one of athletics' brightest lights. His performances were distinguished by both technical perfection and an inherent ability to deal with pressure, attributes that set him apart from many competitors. During this transitional period, he achieved great success

Armand Duplantis biography: The Life of a Pole Vaulting Sensation

through a mix of talent, hard effort, and strategic decision-making.

Along with smashing records, Mondo's shift into professional athletics enabled him to compete in important competitions such as the Diamond League series, which showcases the world's best athletes across multiple disciplines. Competing in these high-stakes scenarios helped him improve his skills while also offering crucial experience that would benefit him in future competitions. Mondo's success was noticed by both fans and the media, and he quickly became one of the most well-known figures in track and field. His captivating attitude and strong performances drew the attention of sponsors and brands wanting to partner with such a powerful athlete.

Armand Duplantis biography: The Life of a Pole Vaulting Sensation

This publicity not only raised Mondo's reputation but also helped improve awareness about pole vaulting as a sport, which is a remarkable accomplishment given its niche status in comparison to other sporting events. Mondo remained grounded and focused on constant growth as he moved forward in his career. He realized that moving on from junior tournaments required accepting new difficulties while being humble, a virtue instilled in him by his family throughout his childhood.

This balance enabled him to be authentic to himself while achieving greatness in pole vaulting. Mondo's journey into professional athletics culminated at the Tokyo 2020 Olympics, which were held in 2021 due to pandemic-related delays. Competing under enormous pressure on such a huge stage, he won gold with a jump of 6.02 meters (19 feet 9 inches), accomplishing a lifetime dream and solidifying his global status as an

Armand Duplantis biography: The Life of a Pole Vaulting Sensation

elite athlete. This victory was more than just about winning; it represented years of effort and hard work culminating in an unforgettable moment that would define his career.

Duplantis's shift to professional athletics was a watershed moment in his quest to become one of the greatest pole vaulters in history. By foregoing academic eligibility after only one year at LSU, he embraced opportunities to focus completely on honing his art while competing at competitive levels around the world. Mondo established himself as a renowned figure in track and field by shattering records and achieving extraordinary feats, including Olympic gold, while also inspiring future generations.

His biography shows how ambition mixed with talent can propel people to tremendous heights,both literally, by clearing vaults above high barriers, and symbolically, by making enduring contributions to their respective sports.

Major Championships and Records

Armand Mondo Duplantis has established himself as a strong force in pole vaulting, winning multiple major championships and setting records. His athletic career has been marked by outstanding performances at all

Armand Duplantis biography: The Life of a Pole Vaulting Sensation

levels, demonstrating his talent and determination to excel in the sport.

Mondo's ascent to notoriety began at a young age, and he swiftly established himself on the international scene. In 2015, at the age of 15, he won the "World Youth Championships" in Cali, Colombia, clearing 5.30 meters (17 feet 4 inches). This triumph not only earned him a gold medal but also set a championship record, establishing him as one of the most promising teenage pole vaulters in history. His performance at this event created the framework for future success and cemented his status as a competitor to watch.

The next year, Mondo continued to impress, winning bronze in the World U20 Championships in Bydgoszcz, Poland. He cleared 5.50 meters (18 feet 0.5 inches), displaying his ability to compete with older athletes and cementing his status as a rising star in the sport. In 2017, Mondo won the European U20 Championship, demonstrating his ongoing growth and development as an elite pole vaulter.

He backed up his success with a spectacular victory at the World U20 Championships in 2018, clearing 5.80 meters (19 feet 0.25 inches). This performance not only earned him another gold medal but also made him the first athlete to reach that height at the U20 level.

As Mondo advanced to senior-level contests, he easily adjusted to the greater level of competition and expectations. His breakthrough came in the "2019 World Championships" in Doha, Qatar, where he earned a silver medal with a 5.97-meter jump (19 feet 7 inches). Competing against seasoned competitors such as Sam Kendricks, Mondo displayed his ability to compete

**Armand Duplantis biography: The Life of a Pole Vaulting
Sensation**

under pressure on the international level. Mondo's first
major win as a senior athlete came at the "2021
European Indoor Championships", where he won gold
with a 6.00-meter leap (19 feet 8.25 inches).

This victory was notable because it demonstrated his
readiness to compete at the highest levels of athletics and
signaled his emergence as one of the world's best pole
vaulters.

One of Mondo's defining moments came during the
Tokyo 2020 Olympics, which were hosted in 2021 due to
pandemic-related delays. He entered this highly
anticipated event as one of the top gold medal
contenders. Mondo performed a spectacular effort,
winning his first Olympic gold medal with a 6.02-meter
jump (19 feet 9 inches). This triumph not only fulfilled a
lifelong desire but also established him as an elite athlete

Armand Duplantis biography: The Life of a Pole Vaulting Sensation

on a global scale. The Olympic victory was very memorable for Mondo because it marked years of hard effort and sacrifice that culminated in an astounding accomplishment. His triumph in Tokyo catapulted him to global recognition and cemented his status as one of history's best pole vaulters.

Mondo's career has also been highlighted by an astounding string of world records that have revolutionized what is possible in pole vaulting. He established his first world record on February 8, 2020, at an indoor tournament in Glasgow, Scotland, clearing 6.17 meters (20 feet 3 inches). This achievement constituted a watershed moment in his career, triggering a chain reaction of record-breaking performances.

Mondo won gold at the "World Athletics Championships" in Eugene, Oregon in July 2022, breaking his world record of 6.21 meters (20 feet 4.5 inches). This was particularly noteworthy because it was his first outdoor world record, demonstrating his ability to execute in a variety of situations and against difficult competition. Later that year, at the European Championships in Munich, Germany, Mondo continued to amaze, shattering the championship record with a jump of 6.06 meters (19 feet 10.5 inches), cementing his domination in the sport. Mondo began the year 2023 on a high note, breaking yet another world record on February 25 at an indoor meet in Clermont-Ferrand, France, clearing an incredible height of 6.22 meters (20 feet 5 inches).

This performance contributed to his impressive list of accomplishments and reflected his unwavering pursuit of excellence. Mondo's most recent world record came on September 17, 2023, during the Prefontaine Classic in

Armand Duplantis biography: The Life of a Pole Vaulting Sensation

Eugene, Oregon, where he cleared an astounding height of 6.23 meters. This performance not only marked his seventh world record but also demonstrated his ability to always push the frontiers of the sport.

Throughout his career, Mondo has acquired an outstanding collection of titles and accolades across many championships, like the 2015 - World U20 Bronze Medalist, 2016 - European U20 Champion, 2017 - World U20 Champion, 2018 - World Championships Silver Medalist, 2019 - European Indoor Champion 2021 - Olympic Champion, Tokyo 2020 - World Champion (Outdoor), 2022 - European Champion, Munich 2022 - World Champion (Outdoor) and Budapest 2023.

In addition to these big wins, Mondo has excelled in Diamond League tournaments, winning multiple titles in consecutive years from 2021 to the present, and has received various honors for his remarkable performance. Mondo's accomplishments have not gone unnoticed in the athletics community or elsewhere; he has been voted World Male Athlete of the Year several times and has won recognition from numerous sporting bodies for his services to athletics. His ability to constantly shatter records while competing at high levels has inspired thousands of young athletes around the world.

Furthermore, Mondo's contribution to pole vaulting goes beyond numbers; his captivating presence and entertaining performances have rekindled interest and passion in the sport. His approachability and humility appeal to fans and aspiring sportsmen alike, making him not only a champion but also a role model in sports.

Mondo continues to compete at elite levels, having just defended his Olympic title in Paris 2024, and it is

Armand Duplantis biography: The Life of a Pole Vaulting Sensation

impossible to predict how many more records or titles he may break or win in the next seasons. His tireless quest for greatness inspires and motivates others who follow in his footsteps.

Armand's career has been distinguished by major championships and record-breaking feats that have set new standards in pole vaulting. From early youth championship victories to Olympic glory and several world records, his journey illustrates what is possible with dedication and hard effort, inspiring future generations along the way.

As he continues to push barriers in athletics today, both literally through heights cleared above high bars and figuratively through long-term impacts produced within their respective sports,Mondo's legacy will undoubtedly last for years to come.

CHAPTER 3: WORLD RECORD

Armand Mondo Duplantis has left an indelible impression on the sport of pole vaulting, not only with his amazing athletic accomplishments but also by continuously breaking world records. His path as a record-breaking athlete began in 2020 and has since evolved, demonstrating his exceptional talent and determination.

Mondo's maiden entry into the world record books was on February 8, 2020, at an indoor event in Torun,

Poland. He cleared 6.17 meters (20 feet 3 inches), breaking the previous mark of 6.14 meters held by French pole vaulter Renaud Lavillenie in 2014. This jump was a watershed moment for Mondo, cementing his place as a key figure in pole vaulting and ushering in a new era for the sport.

Only one week later, on February 15, 2020, Mondo shattered his own freshly created record by clearing "6.18 meters (20 feet 3.25 inches" at an indoor meet in Glasgow, Scotland. This performance not only cemented his title as the world's best pole vaulter, but it also displayed his ability to constantly push the envelope and improve his performances in quick succession.

After a temporary sabbatical from breaking records due to the COVID-19 outbreak, Mondo returned to competition with newfound zeal. On March 7, 2022, he cleared "6.19 meters (20 feet 3.75 inches)" at the World Indoor Championships in Belgrade, Serbia. This jump set his third-world record and cemented his domination in indoor pole vaulting.

Just two weeks later, on March 20, 2022, Mondo reached another milestone by clearing "6.20 meters (20 feet 4 inches)" at an indoor meet in France. This achievement was especially significant since it demonstrated his ability to maintain peak performance levels throughout multiple competitions while constantly raising the bar, literally and figuratively.

On July 24, 2022, during the World Athletics Championships in Eugene, Oregon, Mondo broke the outdoor world record for the first time by clearing 6.21 meters (20 feet 4.25 inches). This feat was historic since it signified a big shift from indoor to outdoor records and

Armand Duplantis biography: The Life of a Pole Vaulting Sensation

demonstrated his versatility as an athlete capable of competing in a variety of conditions. This effort was remarkable not only for its height but also for its time; it occurred during one of athletics' most renowned tournaments, cementing his place as one of the best pole vaulters in history. The atmosphere at Hayward Field was electric with excitement as supporters anticipated Mondo's try at this new height. His successful jump elicited deafening acclaim and cheers from the audience, cementing a historic moment that would be remembered for years.

Mondo continued his series of record-breaking achievements by setting a new world record on February 25, 2023, at an indoor meet in Clermont-Ferrand, France. After knocking the bar on his first two attempts at that height, he cleared "6.22 meters (20 feet 5 inches)" with plenty of room on his third try. This jump cemented his

Armand Duplantis biography: The Life of a Pole Vaulting Sensation

status as one of the greatest pole vaulters in history. This performance showcased his ability to perform under pressure while also demonstrating his technical knowledge of the pole vault. The timing of this jump emphasized its significance; it signified yet another milestone in an already amazing career loaded with accomplishments.

On September 17, 2023, at the Diamond League Final in Eugene, Oregon, Mondo cleared "6.23 meters (20 feet 5¼ inches)". This feat not only added another world record to his resume but also demonstrated his ability to perform under pressure in high-stakes events.

In April of the following year, during the Diamond League competition in Xiamen, China, Mondo beat his record by clearing "6.24 meters (20 feet 5¾ inches)" on April 21. This was his eighth world record overall and

Armand Duplantis biography: The Life of a Pole Vaulting Sensation

demonstrated his relentless pursuit of perfection within the sport.

Mondo broke history again at the Paris Olympics in August of that year, clearing "6.25 meters (20 feet 6 inches)" after previously winning gold with a jump of "6.00 meters" earlier in the competition. This extraordinary performance not only earned him another Olympic title but also made him one of only a few athletes to break a world record at the Olympics, which is a dream come true for any competitor.

Most recently, on August 25, at the Silesia Diamond League meeting in Poland, Mondo raised the bar even higher by clearing "6.26 meters (20 feet and nearly seven inches)", his tenth world record overall and testament to his extraordinary talent and dedication to pushing the limits of pole vaulting.

Armand Duplantis biography: The Life of a Pole Vaulting Sensation

Armand Mondo Duplantis' career through pole vaulting has been nothing short of spectacular, with eleven world records demonstrating not only his incredible athletic talent but also his unwavering quest for excellence in the sport. Each record has strengthened his position as one of history's best pole vaulters, pushing future generations to push their limits and aspire for greatness.

CHAPTER 4:OLYMPIC ACHIEVEMENT

Armand Duplantis has made a huge impact on the
Olympic stage, distinguishing himself as one of the best
pole vaulters in history. His Olympic experience has
been distinguished by amazing performances,
record-breaking accomplishments, and a rising legacy
that resonates around the world.

Mondo Duplantis made his Olympic debut at the "Tokyo
2020 Olympics", which were held in 2021 due to
pandemic-related delays. Mondo entered the men's pole
vault final as a favorite, having already established
himself in world athletics with many junior and senior

Armand Duplantis biography: The Life of a Pole Vaulting Sensation

titles. On August 3, 2021, Mondo gave an outstanding performance, clearing "6.02 meters (19 feet 9 inches)" on his first attempt. This height earned him the gold medal, which marked a watershed moment in his career because it was his first Olympic triumph.

 The triumph was lauded not just for the accomplishment itself, but also for its historical significance: Mondo became the first Swedish pole vaulter to win an Olympic gold medal. The atmosphere during the final was explosive, with both viewers and competitors mesmerized by Mondo's talent and composure. His ability to perform under pressure was clear as he approached each jump with confidence and determination.

After winning gold, Mondo tried three times to shatter his world record of "6.18 meters", but he came up just short. Nonetheless, his accomplishment in Tokyo cemented his reputation as a top-tier athlete and paved the way for future success. Mondo returned to the Olympic stage for the Paris 2024 Olympics, which took place on August 5, 2024. This time, he hoped not just to defend his title, but also to set a new world record on one of athletics' most prestigious venues.

The excitement surrounding his performance was apparent, with fans and fellow competitors eagerly anticipating what he would accomplish. During the final at the Stade de France, Mondo began by clearing "6.00 meters (19 feet 8.25 inches)" easily, earning him another gold medal. This height also surpassed the previous Olympic record of "6.03 meters" achieved by Brazilian Thiago Braz at the 2016 Rio Olympics. With this spectacular jump, Mondo became only the second man in history to win back-to-back Olympic gold medals in

Armand Duplantis biography: The Life of a Pole Vaulting Sensation

pole vaulting, following American hero Bob Richards, who did it in 1952 and 1956.

Mondo's ambitions didn't end there; after winning gold, he increased the bar to "6.10 meters" and cleared it on his first try, setting a new Olympic record in the process. The crowd roared in enthusiasm as he continued to push himself further, hoping to shatter his world record of "6.24 meters", which he had set earlier that year. Mondo encountered difficulties with this try; after two unsuccessful attempts at "6.25 meters" he attacked his final attempt with resolve and attention. The atmosphere was packed with excitement as fans cheered him on. On his final attempt, he soared effortlessly over the bar, clearing "6.25 meters (20 feet 6 inches)", not only setting a world record but also creating an iconic moment in Olympic history.

Armand Duplantis biography: The Life of a Pole Vaulting Sensation

This leap cemented Mondo's place as one of history's best pole vaulters, adding to his athletic legacy. His performance in Paris demonstrated his ability to execute under extreme duress while setting historic records that few sportsmen can match.

Mondo Duplantis' involvement in the Olympics had a significant impact on pole vaulting and athletics in general. His successes have encouraged other young athletes worldwide to follow their aspirations in track and field sports. His commitment to excellence and constant pursuit of progress demonstrate what can be accomplished with hard effort and determination. Furthermore, Mondo's presence at key tournaments has refocused attention on pole vaulting as a discipline, raising its status in global athletics discussions. His ability to regularly smash records while competing

Armand Duplantis biography: The Life of a Pole Vaulting Sensation

against elite athletes has led to comparisons with other sports legends.

Mondo's successes have not only inspired future generations of pole vaulters but have also considerably improved Sweden's sporting reputation. His performance has increased international awareness of Swedish athletics while also instilling pride in home fans.

While Mondo Duplantis' Olympic medals are unquestionably major indicators of accomplishment, they also represent an age of greatness in pole vaulting that prioritizes breaking barriers and redefining limitations. As he continues to compete at the best level, he recently defended both Olympic titles, it is impossible to predict how many more records he will break or championships he will win in the coming seasons.

Armand Duplantis biography: The Life of a Pole Vaulting Sensation

His experience thus far demonstrates how talent mixed with devotion can propel people to amazing heights, both literally, through vaults cleared over high bars, and symbolically, through long-term contributions to their sports.

Armand Mondo Duplantis' Olympic participation has been marked by outstanding performances that have altered pole vaulting standards while motivating future generations. From winning gold medals in Tokyo and Paris to setting world records under extreme duress, his journey serves as a reminder that success is frequently the result of unshakable dedication and passion for one's art. As he prepares for future events, both national and international, Mondo's legacy will increase as he strives for new heights in athletics today.

Gold Medal Performances at Tokyo 2020 and Paris 2024

Armand Mondo Duplantis has cemented his place as one of history's best pole vaulters with his outstanding accomplishments at the Olympic Games. His gold medal victories at the Tokyo 2020 Olympics and the Paris 2024 Olympics demonstrate not just his physical prowess, but also his capacity to perform under pressure on the world's largest stage.

Armand Duplantis biography: The Life of a Pole Vaulting Sensation

Mondo Duplantis made his Olympic debut at the Tokyo 2020 Olympics, which were held in 2021 due to the COVID-19 pandemic. The men's pole vault final was held on August 3, 2021, at Tokyo's National Stadium, with Mondo entering as one of the favorites. Years of hard work, commitment, and a string of record-breaking achievements before the Games had led him to this point. As the competition progressed, Mondo exhibited exceptional talent and poise.

He opened his campaign by effortlessly clearing "5.70 meters (18 feet 8.25 inches)", demonstrating his technical proficiency and confidence. He then increased his height till he reached 6.00 meters (19 feet 8.25 inches). This height not only earned him the gold medal but also set an Olympic record, surpassing the previous record of "6.03 meters" achieved by Brazil's Thiago

Armand Duplantis biography: The Life of a Pole Vaulting Sensation

Braz at the Rio 2016 Olympics. The atmosphere in the final was electrifying, with fans cheering as Mondo made his tries. His triumph was especially notable because it marked the first time a Swedish pole vaulter had won an Olympic gold medal in this event.

The accomplishment reflected years of hard work and demonstrated his outstanding talent. After winning gold with a jump of 6.00 meters, Mondo aimed higher, hoping to surpass his world record of 6.18 meters, set earlier that year in Glasgow. He came near on three attempts but did not clear that height. Nonetheless, his achievement in Tokyo solidified him as a dominant force in pole vaulting and represented a watershed moment in his career. Mondo reflected on his experience with disbelief and excitement, saying, "It's a bizarre feeling... I'm still not sure how to convey it... I've always believed that it will lead me to some wonderful destinations. His victory in Tokyo was more than just winning; it was the realization of a lifelong desire on one of the sport's most prestigious platforms.

Three years later, Mondo returned to the Olympic stage for the Paris 2024 Olympics, which took place on August 5, 2024. This time, he hoped not only to defend his championship but also to create a new world record in front of a boisterous audience at the Stade de France. The excitement surrounding this event was considerable, with fans and fellow athletes eager to see what Mondo might accomplish.

During the final, Mondo began his performance at 5.70 meters, clearing it effortlessly before moving on to 5.80 meters and returning for 5.85 meters, which he also cleared with ease. By this time in the competition, it was obvious that he was in top shape. As he reached 6.00

Armand Duplantis biography: The Life of a Pole Vaulting Sensation

meters, Mondo's confidence shined through; he cleared the height without difficulty, claiming another Olympic gold medal and shattering Thiago Braz's previous Olympic record by seven centimeters. With this accomplishment, he became only the second man in history to win back-to-back Olympic gold medals in pole vaulting, following American Bob Richards in 1952 and 1956.

However, Mondo was not content with merely winning gold; he wanted to make history by breaking his world record of 6.24 meters, which he had set earlier that year in Xiamen, China. After passing 6.00 meters, he upped the bar to 6.10 meters, further distinguishing his already great career. After a good jump of 6.10 meters, Mondo tried for 6.25 meters, one centimeter higher than his current world record. The viewers' enthusiasm grew as they watched him prepare for this daring endeavor.

Armand Duplantis biography: The Life of a Pole Vaulting Sensation

Mondo nearly missed clearing the bar on his first two efforts at 6.25 meters, but he remained calm and concentrated on making improvements for his final attempt.

The atmosphere was packed with expectation as spectators clapped rhythmically in support and sang his name. Mondo ran toward the bar, determined and focused on his final attempt at this historic height. He propelled himself into the air, perfectly twisting his body around the bar without making contact, a feat that drew deafening acclaim from the captivated audience as he landed safely on the mat below. This jump not only set a new world record, but it also crowned him an Olympic champion once more, a moment that summed up years of hard work and dedication coming to fruition on one of athletics' grandest stages.

Armand Duplantis biography: The Life of a Pole Vaulting Sensation

Mondo reflected on his wonderful experience, saying, "What can I say? I recently broke a world record at the Olympics, the largest stage for a pole vaulter... It's one of those things that doesn't feel real, like an out-of-body experience." His win in Paris cemented his legacy in athletics while encouraging future generations of athletes worldwide.

Mondo Duplantis' gold medal exploits in Tokyo and Paris are more than just individual accomplishments; they reflect a period of pole vaulting brilliance that stresses breaking barriers and rewriting limitations in sports history. His achievements have re-energized pole vaulting as a discipline, raising its visibility in global athletics discourse and encouraging countless young athletes around the world to pursue their ambitions in track and field sports.

Armand Duplantis biography: The Life of a Pole Vaulting Sensation

Furthermore, Mondo's ability to execute under duress during these high-stakes tournaments demonstrates not only his athletic abilities but also his mental fortitude, an important trait for success in any sport.

Duplantis has etched his name into Olympic history with spectacular achievements that have altered pole vaulting standards while encouraging future generations along the way. From winning gold medals in Tokyo and Paris to setting world records under extreme duress, his journey serves as a reminder that success is frequently the result of unshakable dedication and passion for one's art.

As he continues to compete at the best level, he recently defended both Olympic titles, it is impossible to predict how many more records he will break or championships he will win in the coming seasons

CHAPTER 5: RECENT COMPETITIONS

The 2024 Lausanne Diamond League, held on August 21, 2024, was a notable event in the sports calendar, especially for pole vaulting fans anxious to watch Armand Mondo Duplantis participate after his outstanding performance in the Paris 2024 Olympics. This meet not only demonstrated Duplantis' continued supremacy in the sport, but it also had several thrilling competitions across several disciplines, attracting the attention of track and field fans all around the world.

 Mondo Duplantis opened the Lausanne Diamond League with a dominant performance in the pole vault.

Armand Duplantis biography: The Life of a Pole Vaulting Sensation

Just over a week after winning gold in the Paris Olympics and setting a world mark of "6.25 meters", Duplantis resumed his winning streak by clearing "6.00 meters" effortlessly. His triumph was won with only four leaps, demonstrating his efficiency and expertise as he cleared heights of 5.62 meters, 5.82 meters, 5.92 meters, and lastly 6.00 meters on his first try.

After winning, Duplantis raised the bar to 6.15 meters in an attempt to set a new meet record. He cleared this height on his third attempt, cementing his place as one of the best pole vaulters in history. The atmosphere during his leaps was electrifying, with people cheering him on as he demonstrated his tremendous talent and commitment. Reflecting on his achievement, Mondo emphasized his excitement: "It's always nerve-racking when you have a tremendous performance like I had at the Olympics. I went out on the track today and I enjoyed it." His ability to remain calm and compete at such a high level right following the Olympics demonstrates his mental toughness and passion for the sport.

The Lausanne Diamond League was not only about Mondo's performance; it also included several other thrilling competitions that enthralled spectators. American pole vaulter Sam Kendricks, who won silver in Paris, placed second to Duplantis once more. Kendricks cleared 5.92 meters on his first try, but labored with three failed efforts at 6.00 meters. His competitive drive and resilience were visible as he attempted to confront Duplantis, but he finally failed.

The competition for third place included a thrilling three-way tie between Norway's Sondre Guttormsen, Australia's Kurtis Marschall, and the Philippines' E.J.

Obiena, all of whom cleared 5.82 meters on their initial tries. This close finish demonstrated the depth of talent in pole vaulting and brought an extra element of excitement to the competition.

Greek pole vaulter Emmanouil Karalis, who won bronze in the Paris Olympics, competed in Lausanne but needed two attempts to clear 5.82 meters, placing sixth overall. His participation emphasized the event's competitive element, as he aimed to improve on prior results.

While Mondo's performance was the evening's highlight, other events received attention. The women's shot put featured remarkable throws from elite competitors, demonstrating their talents and commitment as they contended for the win. 5. Emmanuel Wanyonyi's 800m victory: In another thrilling moment of the competition, Kenyan runner Emmanuel Wanyonyi won the men's

Armand Duplantis biography: The Life of a Pole Vaulting Sensation

800m race in 1:41.11, setting a personal best just days after competing in the Olympics. His triumph heightened the enthusiasm of the evening and proved that many competitors were eager to resume their competitive seasons after their Olympic experiences.

The 2024 Lausanne Diamond League provided an important opportunity for athletes to demonstrate their ability quickly after one of athletics' most famous tournaments, the Olympic Games. For Mondo Duplantis, it was an opportunity to confirm his standing as a world-class athlete while also prolonging his winning streak, which had lasted over 13 months. The meet also showcased how athletes could return to competition mode after a stressful Olympic experience, exhibiting their resilience and dedication to their respective sports. The performances in Lausanne set the tone for future

Armand Duplantis biography: The Life of a Pole Vaulting Sensation

Diamond League events while also presenting fans with exciting moments that honored athletic prowess.

Mondo Duplantis competes in numerous Diamond League events throughout the season, hopes are high for more record-breaking performances and ongoing success. His ability to consistently clear heights exceeding six meters has been a defining feature of his career, and supporters eagerly await what he will accomplish next. The Lausanne Diamond League not only displayed Mondo's exceptional potential but also offered a reminder of the depth of competition in athletics today, displaying both established stars and new prospects eager to make their mark on the sport.

The 2024 Lausanne Diamond League featured a spectacular victory and record-breaking performance by Armand Mondo Duplantis, as well as dramatic

Armand Duplantis biography: The Life of a Pole Vaulting Sensation

competitions across various events that enthralled fans around the world. As competitors continue to compete in this season's Diamond League circuit, each aspiring for greatness, the enthusiasm surrounding track and field is tangible.

Performance Analysis and Competition Results

Armand Mondo Duplantis has regularly excelled in pole vaulting, especially at important contests like the "Tokyo 2020 Olympics" and the "2024 Lausanne Diamond League". His accomplishments demonstrate not only his athletic abilities but also his cerebral fortitude and strategic approach to competition. This examination focuses on the specifics of his performances, including technical issues, competition outcomes, and the broader ramifications of his results.

A historic gold medal performance. Mondo Duplantis went into the Tokyo 2020 Olympics with great expectations after a string of record-breaking

Armand Duplantis biography: The Life of a Pole Vaulting Sensation

performances coming up to the event. On August 3, 2021, he competed in the men's pole vault final, where he cleared 6.02 meters (19 feet 9 inches) on his first attempt. This height earned him the gold medal and made him the only competitor in the tournament to clear six meters, demonstrating his supremacy in the event.

Duplantis' technique excelled throughout the competition. He began at 5.70 meters, easily clearing it before moving on to 5.80 meters and returned for 5.85 meters, which he accomplished with great clearance. His approach was distinguished by a forceful run-up, an explosive take-off, and a seamless transition over the bar, showcasing his perfect technique developed over years of practice. After winning gold, Mondo wanted to better his world record of 6.18 meters, which he had established earlier that year. He came near on three attempts at 6.19 meters, but he did not clear that height.

Armand Duplantis biography: The Life of a Pole Vaulting Sensation

Nonetheless, his feat cemented his place as a dominant figure in pole vaulting and represented a watershed moment in his career.

Duplantis' triumph in Tokyo not only gave him an Olympic championship, but also established him as a favorite in future tournaments, raising expectations for his subsequent achievements.

On August 21, 2024, Duplantis competed in the 2024 Lausanne Diamond League, just over a week after winning the Olympics. This meet allowed him to confirm his pole vaulting dominance shortly after winning the Olympics. Mondo began the tournament with a series of amazing jumps, clearing 5.62 meters, 5.82 meters, and 5.92 meters on his first three attempts before successfully jumping 6.00 meters to win. His ability to execute consistently under duress was clear, as he finished first with only four leaps.

After winning, Duplantis lifted the bar to 6.15 meters, which he cleared on his third attempt, establishing a new meeting record in Lausanne. The audience shouted in enthusiasm as he demonstrated both skill and composure throughout the contest. Mondo's performance in Lausanne demonstrated improved technique and mental preparation since the Olympics. His technique remained consistent, with a strong run-up, precise pole planting, and efficient rotation over the bar, all contributing to excellent jumps that exhibited both power and delicacy. Duplantis' triumph in Lausanne extended a winning streak that spanned over thirteen months, demonstrating not just his physical abilities but also his strategic approach to compete after significant tournaments.

Armand Duplantis biography: The Life of a Pole Vaulting Sensation

Mondo Duplantis' results at the Tokyo Olympics and the Lausanne Diamond League show numerous crucial variables that contributed to his success. His ability to execute precise jumps was key to his success. Each leap is distinguished by a forceful run-up and an explosive take-off, allowing him to maximum height while keeping control of his technique. Competing at the elite level necessitates extraordinary mental fortitude, particularly when confronted with high-pressure events such as Olympic finals or significant tournaments shortly following. Mondo has continually shown the capacity to focus and perform under duress, frequently rising to competitors' challenges. Mondo's decision-making during competitions, such as when to pass heights or attempt record-breaking jumps, demonstrates a strategic approach that enables him to maximize performance while avoiding danger. Also, Maintaining top physical condition is critical for any great athlete, and Mondo's

Armand Duplantis biography: The Life of a Pole Vaulting Sensation

intense training regimen has prepared him well for the endurance and explosive power required in pole vaulting. Coaches, family, and support networks played a critical role in Mondo's success; their encouragement and direction helped shape him into the athlete he is today.

As Mondo Duplantis competes in forthcoming Diamond League tournaments and prepares for future championships, hopes remain high for additional titles won and records broken. His recent accomplishments have set new benchmarks in pole vaulting, inspiring younger athletes while also generating knowledge about the sport on worldwide platforms, an important part of developing future generations of competitors.

Mondo Duplantis' performance analysis from both the Tokyo Olympics and the Lausanne Diamond League

Armand Duplantis biography: The Life of a Pole Vaulting Sensation

demonstrates a remarkable trajectory marked by technical excellence, mental resilience, strategic execution, and unwavering dedication to achieving greatness in athletics today.

CHAPTER 6: TRAINING AND COACHING

Armand Duplantis's incredible pole vaulting journey is inextricably linked to his family's coaching heritage, which has played an important role in defining his athletic career. Growing up in an athletic environment, Mondo was exposed to influences that sparked his interest in sports at a young age. His parents, Greg and Helena Duplantis have substantial athletic backgrounds, giving him a unique basis for his growth as a top pole vaulter.

Greg Duplantis, Mondo's father, competed as a collegiate pole vaulter for the University of Louisiana in Lafayette. His own experiences in the sport provided him with vital insights into the technical aspects of pole vaulting. Greg's mastery of the event's fundamentals enabled him to actively advise Mondo during his early preparation. Greg has been there to teach Mondo the principles of the sport when he first took up a pole.

Greg's coaching technique stressed both technical skill and mental preparedness. He instilled in Mondo the value of visualization and attention, which are critical components for success in high-pressure events. Greg's approach was hands-on; he frequently worked with Mondo in their backyard, organizing practice sessions

Armand Duplantis biography: The Life of a Pole Vaulting Sensation

that allowed his son to experiment and improve his skills. This close coaching setting helped father and son form a strong bond based on mutual respect and common aims.

Mondo's mother, Helena, had a big contribution to his athletic development. She, a former heptathlete and long jumper, contributed to the family dynamic by sharing her competitive sports experiences. Helena did not personally instruct Mondo in pole vaulting, but her athletic background gave him additional support and encouragement throughout his quest. Helena highlighted the value of balance, encouraging Mondo to thrive academically while pursuing his athletic goals. Her influence helped Mondo create a well-rounded approach to competition, helping him to grow not only as an athlete but also as a student and person. This comprehensive viewpoint has been critical in defining Mondo's character and work ethic.

Mondo's siblings also influenced his athletic background. His older brother Andreas was a competitive athlete who participated in a variety of sports, and his younger sister Johanna has also expressed an interest in athletics. Growing up in a sports-focused atmosphere inspired Mondo to strive for excellence while also encouraging healthy rivalry among family members. Mondo's family's support went beyond coaching; they were crucial to his emotional well-being amid both wins and setbacks. Celebrating victories together and offering comfort during losses fostered a nurturing environment in which he could thrive.

As Mondo went through junior contests and established himself on the international scene, he switched from

Armand Duplantis biography: The Life of a Pole Vaulting Sensation

family coaching to working with professional trainers who could provide specialized training for elite-level competition. However, the fundamental talents and mental methods imparted by his parents remained with him throughout the transformation. Even as he progressed into professional sports, Mondo drew on the principles he gained from his family's coaching history.

Greg and Helena emphasized the qualities of hard effort, discipline, resilience, and humility, which have remained important to his approach as he navigates the challenges of competing at the highest level.

Duplantis' familial coaching history has had an impact on both his athletic achievements and his character. The solid familial support structure has provided him with critical skills for success, both on and off the field. As he continues to smash records and win titles, Mondo stays true to the values instilled in him by his parents.

Duplantis' family coaching background helped shape him into one of the greatest pole vaulters of all time. With his father Greg's technical expertise and his mother Helena's holistic approach, Mondo built a solid foundation that has driven him to amazing heights in athletics today.

Training Regimen and Techniques

Armand Mondo Duplantis' training regimen is painstakingly planned to improve his pole vaulting performance by incorporating speed training, strength conditioning, technical drills, and mental preparation. This diversified strategy has helped him evolve into an elite athlete capable of setting world records and winning Olympic gold medals.

Mondo's training methodology is built around the emphasis on speed. Recognizing the importance of speed in pole vaulting, he integrates sprint training into his regimen. Mondo feels that running fast requires rapid training, thus he focuses on high-intensity sprint exercises to improve his acceleration and overall running mechanics. Mondo's sprint training consists of short-distance runs ranging from 30 to 150 meters.

These workouts are designed to increase explosive power and speed while reducing tiredness. He frequently engages in sled pulls and resistance sprints to increase his strength and explosiveness. The idea is to convert this speed into energy on the approach run up to the vault. In addition to regular sprint exercises, Mondo performs drills that imitate the last stages of the pole vault technique. This includes training rapid, strong steps that lead to an explosive take-off. His training focuses on the final three strides of the approach, which must be the most forceful and rapid, ensuring he creates maximum vertical force as he plants the pole.

Technical skills are essential in pole vaulting, and Mondo devotes significant time to honing his technique through targeted drills. He exercises several parts of the vaulting technique, such as the plant, take-off, swing-up, and clearance over the bar. Mondo is focused on completing a flawless plant at the exact time. He practices forcing his leg upward while maintaining his toe pointed to achieve a strong inverted C stance upon takeoff. This technique is critical for producing lift and making a smooth transition into the vault.

Also, The swing-up phase is crucial in translating horizontal speed to vertical lift. Mondo uses drills that emphasize sequential action, such as lifting his legs first to propel his hips higher while remaining aligned with the pole. This technique allows him to maximize energy transmission from the pole while keeping his body tight and under control. To improve his ability to clear heights successfully, Mondo works on arching his torso over the bar while keeping a tight trajectory. He focuses on timing his movements so that he can successfully push against the pole while minimizing air resistance.

Strength training is another important part of Mondo's regimen. He utilizes a variety of exercises designed to increase muscular strength unique to pole vaulting. His exercises include Olympic lifts like cleans and snatches, which help him develop explosive strength in crucial muscle areas for vaulting. In addition to Olympic lifts, Mondo performs plyometric training to improve his explosiveness and agility. Box jumps, depth jumps, and medicine ball throws are all part of his practice, which help him strengthen fast-twitch muscle fibers that are required for power generation during takeoff. Mondo's training program also emphasizes core strength, which adds considerably to vault stability and control. He uses exercises like planks, Russian twists, and leg raises to develop his core muscles.

Recognizing the significance of recovery in maintaining peak performance levels, Mondo adds rest days into his training routine. During competitive seasons, he reduces training volume while focusing on fine-tuning methods and maintaining fitness levels with lighter exercises.

Armand Duplantis biography: The Life of a Pole Vaulting Sensation

Mondo's success is also heavily dependent on mental preparation. He uses visualization techniques to mentally rehearse each phase of the vault before execution. This mental representation allows him to gain confidence and focus during competitions. Mondo also utilizes mindfulness techniques such as meditation and yoga to improve mental clarity and lessen the anxiety associated with high-stakes competitions. This comprehensive strategy keeps him mentally sharp as he navigates the pressures of elite-level athletics.

While Mondo's family provided a solid basis for his early pole vaulting growth, he has also worked with professional instructors who contribute specific expertise and experience to his training program. These instructors assess his technique via video breakdowns and provide comments, allowing him to make the required improvements.

Armand Duplantis biography: The Life of a Pole Vaulting Sensation

Mondo's collaborative relationship with his coaches allows him to consistently improve his talents while responding to new conditions throughout tournaments. This adaptability is critical for success in an event where variables like weather or equipment might affect performance.

Armand's training program is distinguished by its holistic approach, which includes speed training, technical drills, strength conditioning, recuperation measures, and mental preparation. Each component of this regimen helps him perform at an elite level consistently. Mondo has become one of the most accomplished pole vaulters in history thanks to his rigorous attention to detail in all aspects of training, from sprint mechanics to bar clearance tactics. His commitment to improving these skills continues to set

Armand Duplantis biography: The Life of a Pole Vaulting Sensation

new standards in the sport, inspiring future generations of athletes to follow in his footsteps

CHAPTER 7: PERSONAL LIFE

Armand Mondo Duplantis' rise to the status of one of history's greatest pole vaulters is inextricably linked to his family's encouragement and influence. His interactions with his parents, siblings, and extended family have influenced his attitude, work ethic, and approach to both sports and life.

Mondo was born into a family that valued sports as a way of life rather than a pastime. His father, Greg Duplantis, was a former collegiate pole vaulter for the University of Louisiana at Lafayette. Helena, his mother,

Armand Duplantis biography: The Life of a Pole Vaulting Sensation

was also an exceptional athlete, having competed in track and field as a heptathlete and long jumper. This athletic background fostered an environment that pushed Mondo to pursue his passion for sports from a young age. Growing up in Lafayette, Louisiana, Mondo was part of a caring family that appreciated each other's accomplishments.

The Duplantis family stressed hard work, discipline, and perseverance, values that have contributed to Mondo's athletic success. Sports events were frequently the focus of family outings, whether they were competitions or friendly athletic challenges among themselves. These events generated a sense of community and healthy competition, which shaped Mondo's competitive spirit.

Greg and Helena Duplantis have played significant roles in Mondo's life, offering advice and encouragement throughout his sports career. During Mondo's early years, Greg served as his coach, giving him technical knowledge about pole vaulting as well as vital mental techniques for competition. His father's background as a former athlete enabled him to empathize with Mondo's goals while also providing practical advice on overcoming obstacles. Helena's impact supplemented Greg's tutoring technique. While she did not personally coach Mondo in pole vaulting, her athletic expertise provided valuable support and encouragement. Helena emphasized the necessity of balancing academics and sports, making sure Mondo recognized the value of education in addition to his athletic ambitions. This comprehensive approach has contributed to Mondo's well-rounded personality and ability to deal with pressure both on and off the field.

Armand Duplantis biography: The Life of a Pole Vaulting Sensation

Mondo has two siblings: his older brother, Andreas, and his younger sister, Johanna. Andreas has also been interested in athletics; he played a variety of sports throughout his youth and acted as a role model and source of inspiration for Mondo. The brothers' friendship is marked by mutual respect and encouragement; they frequently share training suggestions and cheer each other on during events. Johanna has also expressed an interest in athletics, engaging in a variety of sports at school. The sibling relationship creates a supportive environment in which achievements are celebrated together. The Duplantis family frequently attends each other's events, encouraging one another and emphasizing the value of family support in achieving personal goals.

Mondo has garnered international prominence while simultaneously navigating the complications of romantic relationships. While information regarding his personal

Armand Duplantis biography: The Life of a Pole Vaulting Sensation

life is frequently kept hidden, it is known that he has connections to other athletes and members of the sporting world. These partnerships give him additional levels of support since they recognize the specific hurdles that elite athletes encounter. Having a companion with similar experiences can help you retain equilibrium in the face of competition. It enables Mondo to connect with someone who understands the challenges of training schedules, travel obligations, and the mental fortitude required to perform at a high level.

Mondo's associations extend beyond his immediate family and into the larger sporting community. He has made relationships with other sportsmen who compete in pole vaulting and other track and field events. These relationships build camaraderie among participants with similar goals and provide a network of support during tournaments. Mondo's relationships with coaches, mentors, and other athletes foster an environment in which knowledge is openly exchanged. He frequently interacts with younger athletes who aspire to follow in his footsteps, offering advice based on his experiences and urging them to pursue their objectives aggressively.

As a professional athlete competing at the highest levels around the world, Mondo confronts particular hurdles in combining relationships with training obligations. The demands of his schedule necessitate meticulous planning to ensure he maintains connections with family and friends while still devoting time to training. Mondo frequently emphasizes the value of communication in his relationships, whether with family or friends, particularly during busy competition seasons when travel might cause distance.

Armand Duplantis biography: The Life of a Pole Vaulting Sensation

He prioritizes staying connected via phone calls or video chats whenever possible. Mondo's success has also brought him into contact with many significant personalities in sports media and sponsorships. Building these professional contacts is critical for handling opportunities that come with his profile as a world-class athlete.

Duplantis' family's history of support is visible not only in his accomplishments but also in his personality. His parents' principles of hard work, humility, and resilience continue to influence him as he faces problems on and off the field. As he continues to smash records and win titles on worldwide stages, Mondo is supported by the affection and encouragement of those closest to him. His dedication to retaining strong family relationships while chasing achievement serves as an inspiration to young athletes worldwide.

Armand Duplantis biography: The Life of a Pole Vaulting Sensation

Finally, Armand Mondo Duplantis' familial relationships helped shape him into one of pole vaulting's greatest athletes. With steadfast support from parents Greg and Helena and encouragement from siblings Andreas and Johanna, Mundo's story illustrates how strong familial relationships may generate success while inspiring future generations,

Influence of Duplantis's Upbringing on His Career

Armand Mondo Duplantis' childhood had a significant impact on his development as an elite athlete and the trajectory of his pole vaulting career. Mondo grew up in an athletic family, surrounded by encouragement, support, and a competitive culture that paved the way for his future success.

Mondo grew up in a sports-centric household. His father, Greg Duplantis, was a former collegiate pole vaulter, and his mother, Helena, was a successful heptathlete. This parental background fostered a natural interest in athletics, as Mondo saw firsthand the devotion and passion required to excel in sports. He learned the qualities of hard work, discipline, and tenacity from his

Armand Duplantis biography: The Life of a Pole Vaulting Sensation

everyday encounters with his parents, who acted as both role models and mentors. The Duplantis family valued more than just athletic involvement; they valued excellence. Athletic events, whether in the form of competitions or casual sporting activities, were frequently the focus of family trips. This atmosphere instilled in Mondo a competitive attitude while also teaching him the value of teamwork and togetherness.

Mondo first tried pole vaulting at the age of three. His father constructed a temporary pole vault facility in their garden, allowing Mondo to practice the sport before fully understanding its complexities. This early exposure gave him a rare opportunity to learn key skills at a young age. The lighthearted nature of these early experiences helped foster a fondness for the sport that would last into his later years. Mondo's skills improved as he advanced through childhood, thanks to his father's tutelage.

Armand Duplantis biography: The Life of a Pole Vaulting Sensation

Greg's coaching strategy emphasizes technical proficiency while pushing Mondo to experiment with different vaulting techniques and approaches. This hands-on coaching method enabled Mondo to build a solid foundation in pole vaulting mechanics while also encouraging innovation in his training.

Mondo's family's support has helped shape his career path. His parents emphasized the importance of education in addition to athletics, making sure he understood the necessity of balance in life. This comprehensive approach enabled Mondo to flourish academically while also following his passion for pole vaulting. His family's encouragement went beyond basic involvement; they celebrated each victory together and comforted him after setbacks. This emotional support

Armand Duplantis biography: The Life of a Pole Vaulting Sensation

has been critical in keeping Mondo motivated and resilient throughout his athletic career.

Mondo's siblings also helped to create a competitive but supportive environment. Growing up with an older brother, Andreas, who also participated in athletics, instilled a spirit of healthy competition in the family. This dynamic inspired Mondo to push himself further while teaching him crucial lessons in sportsmanship and respect for others.

 Mondo's background instilled in him the mental strength required for success at the highest levels of the sport. His parents taught him how to handle pressure, which is a crucial ability for any athlete striving for success. They emphasized the significance of staying focused throughout competitions and envisioning success before climbing difficult heights. This mental preparation was especially noticeable at high-stakes events like national championships and international competitions. Mondo learned early on how to convert nerves into positive energy, allowing him to perform at his peak when it counted the most. His ability to remain calm under pressure has been a defining feature of his career.

Growing up in an athlete-rich environment gave Mondo multiple role models that pushed him to strive for excellence. In addition to his parents, he admired renowned figures in the sport of pole vaulting, such as Renaud Lavillenie, who set world records throughout his career. Meeting Lavillenie as a young athlete created a lasting influence on Mondo, inspiring him to mimic his dedication while creating his style. These meetings reinforced the belief that success can be achieved through hard effort and determination, principles that Mondo has followed throughout his career.

Armand Duplantis biography: The Life of a Pole Vaulting Sensation

 As Mondo progressed from junior tournaments to elite-level events, he brought with him not only technical skills but also the ideals established by his upbringing. His early victories at youth competitions paved the way for future success on greater stages. The confidence garnered from winning tournaments during his formative years influenced Mondo's competitive spirit as he confronted increasingly difficult opponents at the adult level. He tackled each new tournament with the idea that he could achieve, a mindset shaped by the support and encouragement he got from family members along the way.

Mondo's upbringing instilled in him a desire for continual improvement, a philosophy that motivates him to always better his technique and performance. His parents encouraged him to pursue this goal by

Armand Duplantis biography: The Life of a Pole Vaulting Sensation

emphasizing that success is more than just winning; it is about personal growth and development. This concept has motivated Mondo to seek out opportunities for learning and growth throughout his career. He actively engages with coaches who provide specialized instruction while remaining open to feedback and constructive criticism, which reflects the principles instilled in him during his upbringing.

Duplantis' upbringing has had an impact not only on his achievements but also on his personality. The solid familial support structure has provided him with critical skills for success, both on and off the field. As he continues to smash records and win titles in the international arena, Mondo is supported by the affection and encouragement of those closest to him. His dedication to retaining strong family relationships while

Armand Duplantis biography: The Life of a Pole Vaulting Sensation

chasing achievement serves as an inspiration to young athletes worldwide.

 In summary, Armand Mondo Duplantis' upbringing has had a profound impact on his pole vaulting career through early exposure to athletics, supportive family dynamics, mental resilience training, role model inspiration, and a commitment to continuous improvement, all of which have contributed to his development into one of history's greatest pole vaulters

CHAPTER 8: MEDIA PRESENCE AND POPULARITY

Duplantis has developed as a renowned figure in the world of athletics, not only for his outstanding exploits in pole vaulting but also for his influential social media presence and engaging public image. Mondo's impact as a world record-breaking athlete and winner of important trophies extends beyond the competitive arena, impacting how spectators perceive him and the sport of pole vaulting.

Armand Duplantis biography: The Life of a Pole Vaulting Sensation

Mondo's social media presence has developed tremendously along with his sporting career. Platforms like Instagram, Twitter, and TikTok have enabled him to engage with followers all over the world, providing insight into his life as an elite athlete. His accounts are jam-packed with information that includes not only his training routines and competitive highlights but also personal moments that resonate with followers.

One of the most important parts of Mondo's social media approach is authenticity. He opens up about his life, including behind-the-scenes footage from tournaments, training sessions, and encounters with family and friends. This candor has endeared him to fans, allowing them to see the person behind the athlete. Mondo has built a loyal following by portraying himself as personable and down-to-earth, and they value both his physical prowess and charm.

Armand Duplantis biography: The Life of a Pole Vaulting Sensation

Mondo's ability to make fascinating content has helped him gain fame on social media. He frequently participates in challenges or trends that appeal to younger audiences, demonstrating his humorous side while remaining focused on athletics. For example, recordings of him completing viral challenges or sharing amusing moments from contests have received a lot of attention, increasing his and the sport's profile.

One memorable viral scene came during the 2024 Paris Olympics, when Mondo celebrated his gold medal victory by rushing towards his partner, model Desiré Inglander, directly after clearing a height of 6.25 meters. The passionate display captured on camera moved viewers and immediately spread throughout social media channels, cementing Mondo's standing as a beloved character in athletics.

Armand Duplantis biography: The Life of a Pole Vaulting Sensation

As Mondo's public image has increased, so have the prospects for brand collaborations and endorsements. He has collaborated with prominent corporations like as Puma and Red Bull, using his profile as a great athlete to promote products that reflect his ideals. These agreements not only provide financial support but also raise his profile in the sports sector. Through these relationships, Mondo has been able to reach a larger audience while also promoting pole vaulting. His endorsements frequently include visually appealing content that showcases both the joy of athletics and the lifestyle that comes with being a professional athlete.

This crossover between sports and lifestyle appeals to fans who want to be like their favorite athletes both on and off the field.

Armand Duplantis biography: The Life of a Pole Vaulting Sensation

Mondo's public presence is defined by a combination of humility, confidence, and charisma. Despite his physical excellence, he is frequently described as friendly and down-to-earth. This mix makes him relatable to followers who love both his achievements and his personality. His contacts with fans on social media serve to reinforce this persona. Mondo often interacts with his followers, reacting to comments and posting user-generated content that recognizes their support for him. This level of involvement fosters a sense of community among supporters, encouraging devotion and admiration for the player.

Similarly, Mondo's ability to express his experiences, whether discussing competitive challenges or offering insights into his training regimen, has established him as a role model for aspiring athletes. He emphasizes the value of hard effort and dedication while keeping

Armand Duplantis biography: The Life of a Pole Vaulting Sensation

grounded in reality, motivating others to pursue their passions fiercely.

Mondo's effect extends beyond personal branding; it has far-reaching repercussions for the sport of pole vaulting. He has contributed to the rise of pole vaulting's profile in athletics by boosting awareness through social media. His record-breaking performances have garnered notice from mainstream media outlets, increasing interest in the event among casual sports fans. Mondo's increased visibility in pole vaulting has the potential to motivate future generations of athletes to participate. By displaying its thrill through engaging content and personal tales, he inspires young people to pursue their athletic potential, ultimately contributing to the expansion of pole vaulting at the grassroots level.

Armand Duplantis biography: The Life of a Pole Vaulting Sensation

While Mondo reaps the benefits of being a public figure, he also faces the problems that come with celebrity. The pressure to perform regularly at high levels can be daunting; nevertheless, he manages this strain using mental preparation tactics learned during his upbringing. His ability to convert external expectations into motivation rather than stress enables him to remain focused during competitions.

Mondo recognizes that social media can sometimes intensify scrutiny; yet, he is devoted to remaining authentic to himself while navigating these hurdles. By focusing on internal improvement rather than external validation, he develops resilience, which allows him to thrive in both competitive and public settings.

As Duplantis continues to smash records and reach new milestones in pole vaulting, his social media presence is

Armand Duplantis biography: The Life of a Pole Vaulting Sensation

expected to rise even more. With further tournaments on the horizon, including potential appearances in future Olympic Games, he will have numerous opportunities to interact with fans while promoting himself and the sport he enjoys.

Armand's social media presence and public persona have considerably influenced how he is seen as an athlete today. Through genuine involvement with fans and compelling content production, he has positioned himself as not only one of history's best pole vaulters but also an important character capable of influencing future generations.

Comparisons to Other Athletes

Duplantis has often been compared to other elite
athletes, both in pole vaulting and in other sports. These
similarities reflect not just his exceptional talent, but also
his influence on the sport and capacity to inspire future
generations of sportsmen.

One of the most common similarities made to Mondo
Duplantis is with famous pole vaulter Sergey Bubka.
Bubka, a Ukrainian athlete, dominated the pole vaulting
scene in the 1980s and 1990s, setting an amazing world
record of 6.14 meters that lasted over two decades. His
creative skills and competitive drive transformed the
sport, making him a household brand. Mondo's
ascension in pole vaulting has been compared to Bubka's

career because of their ability to continually shatter records. Mondo has already broken his world record several times, surpassing heights that many considered unachievable.

Both athletes have displayed great technical ability, mental toughness, and a never-ending quest for excellence. However, whereas Bubka's record-breaking performances were typified by progressive gains over time, Mondo's approach has been marked by a series of tiny advancements, often breaking records by a single centimeter. Some critics believe Mondo's unique style might be further polished for even greater heights, with the conjecture that if he improves his approach, he could one day clear 6.40 meters.

Renaud Lavillenie, another notable figure in pole vaulting history, is a French athlete. Lavillenie was the

Armand Duplantis biography: The Life of a Pole Vaulting Sensation

first guy to break Bubka's long-held world record, reaching 6.16 meters in 2014. He has dominated the sport, winning multiple titles, including an Olympic gold medal at the 2012 London Olympics. Comparisons between Mondo and Lavillenie frequently center on their opposing methods and approaches to competitiveness. While both athletes have exceptional technical abilities, Mondo is noted for his explosive strength and speed during the approach phase, which has led to his ability to reach heights above those of Lavillenie in his heyday. Lavillenie praised Mondo's accomplishments and recognized him as a worthy successor in the sport. Their rivalry has given interest to tournaments, with fans looking forward to seeing the two athletes battle against one another.

American pole vaulter Sam Kendricks is another well-known competitor who has frequently been

Armand Duplantis biography: The Life of a Pole Vaulting Sensation

compared to Mondo Duplantis. Kendricks is a two-time world champion and Olympic winner renowned for his consistency and fierce drive. He won silver in the Tokyo 2020 Olympics and has been a dominant figure in international pole vaulting competitions. The rivalry between Mondo and Kendricks exemplifies two distinct approaches to the sport: Mondo frequently pushes the boundaries with record-breaking attempts, whereas Kendricks represents dependability and consistency in competition.

Their opposing styles generate an exciting dynamic whenever they compete at large competitions. Kendricks himself has spoken about the burden of competing against someone as good as Mondo: "I'm like a small cog in Mondo's life," he joked after losing against him in Paris 2024. This recognition illustrates not just Kendricks' admiration for Mondo, but also how

Armand Duplantis biography: The Life of a Pole Vaulting Sensation

Duplantis' domination can eclipse even great sportsmen like Kendricks.

Beyond pole vaulting, Mondo Duplantis has been compared to other sports icons from a variety of disciplines. His charisma, athleticism, and marketability have led some observers to compare him to basketball player Timothée Chalamet and soccer star Lionel Messi, athletes who have transcended their sports by combining outstanding abilities with appealing public personas.

The similarity to Timothée Chalamet arises from their shared appeal as young idols who captivate audiences both on and off the field. Chalamet's rise in Hollywood echoes Mondo's rise in athletics; both are seen as representatives of their respective fields, exuding youthful excitement while attaining exceptional success at a young age. Similarly, comparisons to Messi

Armand Duplantis biography: The Life of a Pole Vaulting Sensation

underline Mondo's ability to execute under pressure while constantly producing outstanding results. Both athletes are known for their uncompromising dedication to their art, which inspires admirers all around the world.

Mondo Duplantis' comparisons to other athletes serve not just as benchmarks for his success, but also as sources of encouragement for aspiring athletes all across the world. By setting new standards in pole vaulting, just like Bubka did in his day, Mundo inspires future competitors to push their limitations while pursuing success in their various sports. His ability to break records inspires future generations to dream big and strive for greatness, supporting the notion that with dedication, hard work, and tenacity, anything is possible in sports.

Armand Duplantis biography: The Life of a Pole Vaulting Sensation

Duplantis stands out among elite athletes not just for his outstanding achievements, but also for comparisons to other pole vaulting legends and beyond. Whether drawing similarities to Sergey Bubka's historic supremacy or noting battles with Sam Kendricks and Renaud Lavillenie, Mondo's career continues to shape notions of what is possible in pole vaulting today.

Chapter 9: FUTURE PROSPECT

Armand Mondo Duplantis continues to dominate the world of pole vaulting, with his sights set on a series of upcoming competitions that will cement his legacy in the sport. With a track record of breaking records and winning titles, Mondo's future goals are bold but grounded in the hard work and dedication that have defined his career thus far.

Mondo's primary ambition is to continue to smash world records. Having already achieved several records throughout his career, most recently clearing 6.26 meters, he hopes to continue pushing the limits of pole vaulting. His objective is not just to beat existing records, but also to set new standards that will inspire future generations of athletes. Mondo prioritizes consistency throughout tournaments. While he has shown extraordinary talent and skill, he understands that continuously performing at high levels can be difficult owing to a variety of factors such as weather or competition pressure. By focusing on consistency, he intends to establish himself as a dependable competitor capable of consistently providing exceptional outcomes.

As he trains for upcoming events like the World Athletics Indoor events, defending trophies is crucial. Mondo recognizes that maintaining championships demands not just physical preparation but also mental fortitude, an area in which he excels owing to his upbringing and training schedule. Mondo tries to inspire young athletes through his performance and public

Armand Duplantis biography: The Life of a Pole Vaulting Sensation

persona, in addition to his successes. By participating in local events such as the Mondo Classic and communicating with followers on social media channels, he hopes to inspire aspiring pole vaulters to chase their dreams fiercely.

He aims to leave a lasting legacy in athletics as he moves forward in his career. He wants to be recognized not only for breaking records and winning medals but also as an ambassador for pole vaulting, the sport that turned him into the person he is today. The future contests will have a significant impact not only on Mondo's immediate athletic ambitions but also on his long-term legacy in pole vaulting. Each tournament allows him to exhibit his abilities while competing against some of the world's greatest athletes.

Armand Duplantis biography: The Life of a Pole Vaulting Sensation

Likewise, these tournaments allow Mondo to build on prior triumphs, generating excitement among spectators and increasing interest in pole vaulting as a sport. His accomplishments have the potential to raise athletic awareness and inspire young athletes around the world.

Armand Mondo Duplantis' next competitions will influence both his immediate ambitions and long-term dreams in pole vaulting. With aspirations ranging from breaking world records and defending titles to inspiring future generations, Mondo stays devoted to greatness as it faces new challenges.

Potential for Further Records and Achievements

Armand has already established himself as one of history's best pole vaulters, but the prospect of breaking more records and achieving new heights remains a compelling component of his career. With great talent, hard training, and a robust support system, Mondo is well-positioned to continue pushing the limits of pole vaulting.

One of the defining features of Mondo's success has been his dedication to perfecting his technique. Pole vaulting is a highly technical sport in which tiny changes can result in big performance gains. Mondo's ability to evaluate and alter his technique has played an important role in his record-breaking jumps. As he continues to train with experienced instructors, Mondo is likely to

Armand Duplantis biography: The Life of a Pole Vaulting Sensation

focus on certain parts of his technique that can be improved further. This involves honing his approach run, take-off technique, and swing-up phase, all of which are key components for reaching new heights. The relentless quest for technical excellence keeps him at the forefront of the sport.

Mondo's physical conditioning is critical to his chances of setting future records. His training regimen includes strength training, speed work, and plyometric activities to improve explosive power, which is important for successful pole vaulting. Mondo may experiment with improved strength training approaches or innovative conditioning strategies as his athletic career progresses. He can improve his capacity to produce lift during jumps by focusing on fast-twitch muscle fiber development and general explosiveness.

Armand Duplantis biography: The Life of a Pole Vaulting Sensation

Also, athletic longevity depends on maintaining optimum physical condition. Mondo's commitment to recovery strategies, such as adequate diet, rest, and injury prevention, will be critical as he navigates the demands of elite racing in the coming years. The mental side of competitiveness cannot be stressed when analyzing Mondo's potential for additional success. His background developed in him a strong sense of mental resilience, which he uses to efficiently deal with pressure during competition. Maintaining focus and composure will be crucial as he faces more elite rivals and high-pressure circumstances.

Mondo's participation in large contests has provided him with great coping mechanisms for stress and anxiety. He has shown the capacity to turn external pressures into drive, which will help him set new marks. Mondo can gain a competitive advantage by continuing to improve

Armand Duplantis biography: The Life of a Pole Vaulting Sensation

his mental toughness through visualization techniques and mindfulness practices.

The competitive scene in pole vaulting is constantly changing, with young talents challenging established athletes like Mondo. Rivals like Sam Kendricks and Chris Nilsen are formidable competitors who have continually pushed one other to greater heights. The presence of powerful competition can motivate Mondo to improve his performance. Healthy competition frequently results in record-breaking performances across the board.

The drive to surpass competitors might motivate athletes to push their capabilities beyond what they thought feasible. As Mondo fights against these great individuals, the likelihood of him and his competitors setting new marks increases.

Armand Duplantis biography: The Life of a Pole Vaulting Sensation

Advances in technology have also influenced athletic performance in a variety of sports, including pole vaulting. Equipment innovations, such as advanced-material poles or footwear enhancements, can help an athlete reach new heights. Mondo has already benefited from advanced equipment created exclusively for elite athletes. As technology advances, he may gain access to ever more advanced equipment, which could contribute to increased performance metrics. Keeping up with these improvements will allow him to make use of any new tools that become available for maximizing his jumps.

Access to high-quality training facilities is another element that influences Mondo's potential for future success. Training at elite locations with cutting-edge infrastructure allows athletes like Mondo to fine-tune their skills while reducing injury concerns. Mondo frequently trains at facilities that provide ideal circumstances for pole vaulting practice, giving him numerous possibilities for repetition while experimenting with various techniques. Continued access to such conditions will be critical as he strives to shatter records and set new benchmarks.

While breaking records remains a key part of Mondo's ambitions, he also has broader goals in athletics. His performances have inspired future generations of competitors and promoted pole vaulting as a sport around the world. Mondo hopes that by participating in community activities and communicating with young athletes on social media platforms, he will inspire others to pursue their dreams ruthlessly, regardless of their sport of choice. His dedication to encouraging interest in

Armand Duplantis biography: The Life of a Pole Vaulting Sensation

sports benefits not only pole vaulting but also the whole sporting culture.

As Mondo proceeds on his path to greater success, thoughts about his legacy will become increasingly significant. Establishing himself as one of the all-time greats entails more than just breaking records; it also includes how he influences the game and inspires others along the road. Mondo's legacy will be defined by both his athletic achievements and his work as a pole vaulting ambassador, which allows him to advocate for young athletes while also encouraging inclusion in sports. By focusing on these bigger goals in addition to record-breaking aims, he can make a long-term influence that goes far beyond personal achievements.

Duplantis still has a lot of ability to break records and accomplish even more. Continuous technique progress,

Armand Duplantis biography: The Life of a Pole Vaulting Sensation

dedication to physical training, mental toughness under duress, and healthy rivalries have set the platform for exciting advancements in the future. Mondo's career demonstrates how genius combined with hard work can propel someone to great height.

CONCLUSION

Armand Mondo Duplantis is at the peak of pole vaulting, a sport he has not only excelled at but also altered via his remarkable accomplishments and charismatic presence. As we reflect on his journey, it is evident that Mondo's tale is one of tenacity, determination, and an unshakable love of sports. His journey from a young boy practicing in his garden to becoming a two-time Olympic champion and world record holder demonstrates the enormous impact of his upbringing, training, and family support.

Mondo's career has been defined by several exceptional achievements. He has broken records with a consistency that few athletes can match, raising the standard not only for himself but for future generations of pole vaulters. His global records, most recently clearing 6.26 meters demonstrate his technical ability and physical strength.

Each record-breaking performance has been accompanied by a sense of drama and excitement, enthralling audiences around the world and raising the popularity of pole vaulting as a competitive sport. The importance of his family cannot be emphasized. Mondo was raised in an athletic household, and his parents recognized the demands of competitive sports. His father, Greg, was an excellent coach and mentor, and his mother, Helena, fostered a sense of balance between academics and sports. This strong familial support system has helped shape Mondo's character and work ethic, enabling him to handle the stresses of elite competition with elegance and perseverance. Mondo's public presence strengthens his legacy.

Armand Duplantis biography: The Life of a Pole Vaulting Sensation

Through social media participation and dynamic conversations with followers, he has become a pole vaulting ambassador, inspiring numerous young athletes to pursue their goals. His ability to connect with audiences on a human level, revealing both his accomplishments and his problems, has won him fans all over the world. This connection extends beyond the sport, making Mondo an accessible character who epitomizes the spirit of determination and excellence.

 Mondo's goals for future competitions remain ambitious. He hopes to smash even more records while continuing to inspire others with his performances.

Duplantis is more than just a champion; he is a transformative figure in pole vaulting whose legacy will be felt for years to come. His journey exemplifies what it

Armand Duplantis biography: The Life of a Pole Vaulting Sensation

means to strive for greatness: combining skill with hard work, and enthusiasm with discipline. As he continues to push the frontiers of the sport, Mondo serves as a beacon for aspiring athletes worldwide, reminding them that with commitment and support, they, too, can reach great heights. The world eagerly awaits what this incredible athlete can accomplish next as he continues to reinvent the limits of pole vaulting.